Paradox

Basya Penn

BookLeaf
Publishing

India | USA | UK

Presentation by *BookLeaf Publishing*

Web: www.bookleafpub.com

E-mail: info@bookleafpub.com

ISBN: 9789357612111

First edition 2021

DEDICATION

To my mom, for always being my biggest cheerleader.

PREFACE

There is a pattern in these pages. Each poem leads to the next with a purpose designed to bring the pain and positivity together with grace. I hope that pattern is as healing to you as it is to me.

Breathe

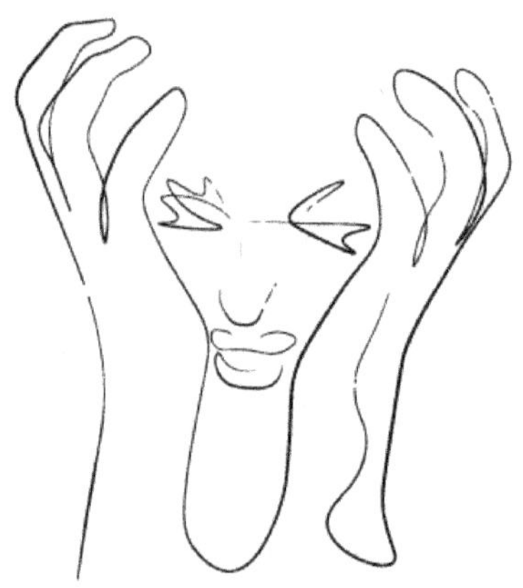

The room fills up with people,
And I hold my breath.
Words and laughter fill the air,
And I hold my breath.

The people speak of trivial things,
And I hold my breath.
Of appearances and pretenses,
And I hold my breath.

They laugh devoid of all truth,
And I hold my breath.

They smile with empty eyes,
And I hold my breath.

As I unstiffen and realign myself,
I let go of my breath.
I walk over to a group and ask,
"Does it hurt to breathe?"

They look at me confusedly amused,
As I breathe carefully.
Upon questions of clarification,
I breathe in and begin to say:

"Do you feel the weight around you,
With every breath you take?
Do you feel the pressure of the façade,
That you're forced to undertake?

"When you hear yourself referred to,
Or see your reflection in a mirror,
Do you feel content with where you are,
Or feel your purpose is any nearer?

"Doesn't it get pretty effortless,
To forget our reason why?
And get caught up in all the details,
To learn simply what to reply?

"The rule book of life can get pretty basic,

If we choose to mask our essence,
It's becoming just scripts, props, and money,
With complete acquiescence.

"It just seems quite painful,
To simply just breath,
With no rationale or premise, so I ask,
Does it hurt to breathe?"

As they stand aghast before me,
Unsure of how to breathe,
They sputter about "chilling out,"
And "breathing more deeply."

As I walk back to my bench slowly,
And I hold my breath,
I sit and hear the laughter resume,
And I hold my breath.

Fear

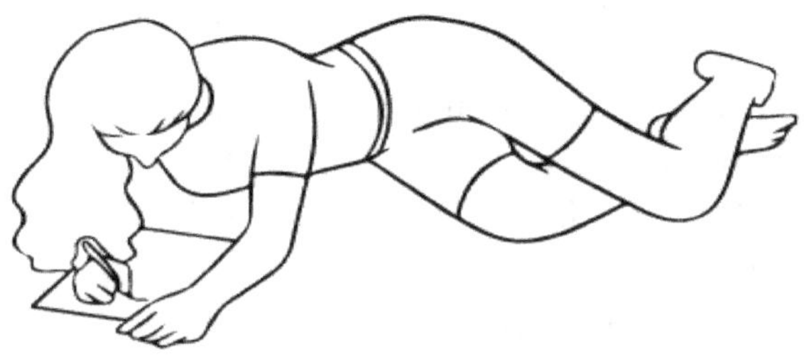

Dearest Fear Within Me,
I just wanted
to let you know,
I'll be limiting our talks
from now on,
While I let
my inner courage grow.
Just recently
I began to notice,
More profoundly
than ever before,
That our discussions
are not in my favor,
And tend to be more
than I care to endure.
You push me

to dwell on anxieties,
And the outcomes
of all my regrets,
When pure joy
comes with mystery,
And not knowing
what'll happen next.
When a bird is learning
to open its wings,
And conquer its fears
of flying high,
The first step is to climb
to the very top,
And the last is to let go
and just try.
I may not be
quite so capable,
Or so charming,
that may be true,
But what I've come
to understand,
Is no one cares
except for you.

The House

Isn't it strange how a house,
Always looks so calm and serene,
When the majority of our lives,
Transpires behind the scene.

A glorious entity of tranquility,
With barbed wire all around,
No reason to escape this place,
From the lovely, fortified ground.

Inside the walls covered with pictures,
People smile from ear to ear,
Though if one would look more closely,
Each pair of eyes are quite austere.

The silent echo of serenity,

Bouncing off of every guise,
From secrecy to suppression,
The peace feels like endless sighs.

On the rare occasion of a visit,
From a friend or perhaps comrade,
The inside is scrubbed of all ill-will,
No sense of any façade.

One may say why emphasize tears,
When there are smiles to mask it all,
As the children in the house grow silent,
And deteriorate as each builds their wall.

So the people in the house stay quiet,
As they go on with their merry life,
Doors shut tight and curtains drawn,
Unable to discern joy from strife.

Isn't it strange how a house,
Always looks so calm and serene,
When the majority of our lives,
Transpires behind the scene.

Paradox

I asked her to explain herself,
As I fixed my glasses on my nose.
She fidgeted and sighed and replied,
"I'm a paradox."

I pursed my lips once again,
I tried reading her countenance.
Expressionless. I read my notes:
"I'm a paradox."

"In what way are you paradoxical?"
I tried, hoping to wiggle into her thoughts.
She smiled brightly with those empty eyes.
She's a paradox.

She began to explain how she feels,
The way she occasionally owns the whole
world,
And how she sometimes embodies the dust.

"I'm a paradox."

She explained how her sadness doesn't make
sense,
Because she can see at night, no matter how
dark,
And that nothing is quite too scary for her,
"I'm a paradox."

She told me that she can see across oceans,
That she never cries, even when she does.
She can count the stars with her eyes closed.
"I'm a paradox."

She told me how she can fly over mountains,
And swim through rivers and seas.
She can jump across the world and back.
"I'm a paradox."

She told me about her adventures Alone,
And she told me about her journeys with Others.
She doesn't see their purpose but needs them.
"I'm a paradox."

She told me that if it's important you'll do it,
But nothing is of true value out there.
She's never done anything that matters.
"I'm a paradox."

I told her about the remedy,
The solution to quiet her mind.
She realized what it meant,
She won't be a paradox.

With the lows come the highs,
With the beauty comes the pain,
With sunrise comes the promise of sunset,
"I'm a paradox."

She refused the antidote to her pain,
She'd prefer to live with the beauty,
Even if that means surviving the lows,
Because she's a paradox.

Home

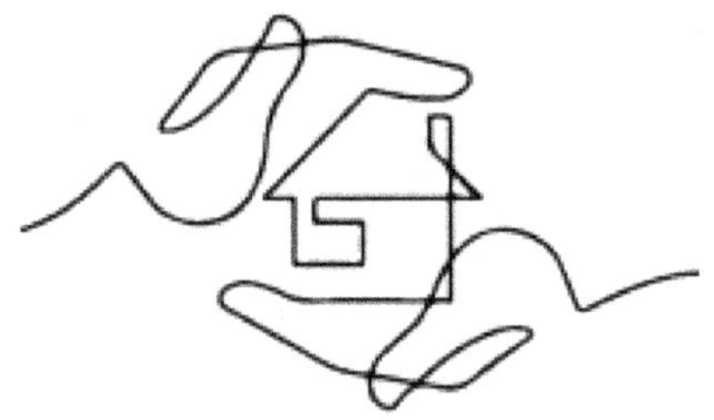

I carry it in my pocket,
So it's never too far away.
That feeling of stability,
It's what I call Home.

It tells me I'm not alone,
To never be afraid.
The energy that keeps me safe,
It's what I call Home.

It keeps me tethered to the ground,
And balanced within extremes.
That ethereal energy,
It's what I call Home.

It whispers comfort in my ear,
And places ease in my step.
It allows me to journey freely,
It's what I call Home.

I bring it with me when I'm sad,
And when I'm afraid.
It tells me I'm my own escape,
It's what I call Home.

I've never had a physical entity,
That I could call "My Home."
It remains nothing but a mindset,
It's what I call Home.

To be pulled to a location,
Seems bothersome at best.
To be whole unto myself,
It's what I call Home.

I carry it in my pocket,
So it's never too far away.
That feeling of stability,
It's what I call Home.

Busy

He's busy with his errands,
But he'll be back very soon,
After all, he really loves me.
He promised, he cares.

He's coming when he's finished,
With his real responsibilities,
After all, I can always trust him.
He promised, he cares.

An emergency came up,
But next he'll be at my side,
After all, I'm most important.
He promised, he cares.

He had to make a stop,
He got tired, he's only human,
After all, I can understand that.
He promised, he cares.

He's coming when he can,
He had a long, hard day,
After all, I'm too naive to get it.
He promised, he cares.

He won't be able to make it today,
Something else came up,
After all, I should care for myself.
He promised, he cared.

Forgive

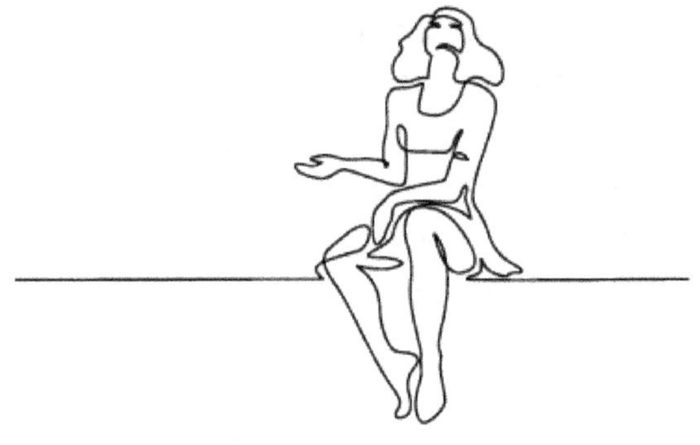

He wrote a rulebook for her to follow,
As clear as a crystal ball.
She read it through like literature,
But didn't use it for her wrongs.
He sighed and shrugged it off,
"I forgive all you have done."

He crafted her world in beautiful knots,
With a labyrinth to finish off the test.
She gave up when it began to get tough,
Kicking and screaming at the offense.
He sighed and shrugged it off.
"I forgive all you have done."

He dispersed her favorite pastimes,
Around her very dearest treasures.

She used them up thanklessly,
Allowing her ego in the way of logic.
He sighed and shrugged it off.
"I forgive all you have done."

He tried to show her the light of truth,
Instead of the fleeting twinkle of despair.
She chose to dabble in the darkness,
Without focusing on the truth.
He sighed and shrugged it off.
"I forgive all you have done."

He loved her with his entire being,
And that was the meaning of forgiveness.
She reached out and felt his hand,
As she reached inward and felt the truth,
She looked up and finally saw him,
As she said the words, "I love you, I'm sorry."
He smiled and shrugged it off.
"I forgive all you have done."

Mania

I step out in the garden,
Among the flowers of demise,
As the wildlife begins to sing and scream,
At last, chaotic and free.

I kneel down to the ground,
Feeling the earth's energy,
I inhale power and exhale strength,
At last, chaotic and free.

I walk out into the world,
To the whispers closing in on me,
They tell me to run and frolic and hide,
At last, chaotic and free.

I continue on my path,
Ignoring the cries and screams,

Urgent demands, shouts, and whims,
At last, chaotic and free.

I stop and sit on the floor,
Anything to shut it all out,
Trying to decipher truth from the lies,
At last, chaotic and free.

I leap up suddenly,
Realizing I can do anything,
I have unlimited capabilities.
At last, chaotic and free.

I begin to run ceaselessly,
Thinking of eternal vitality,
I contain all the souls of the universe.
At last, chaotic and free.

I close my eyes as I fly,
With my sword and my throne,
I am fearless and invincible.
At last, chaotic and free.

Crystal and Stone

As the property of no one,
I am of the elements of the earth.
A pure holistic form,
I am crystal and stone.

I heal and align,
The deepest suffering and pain.
My aura is uniquely mine,
I am crystal and stone.

I shine with brilliant force,
No one can omit my strength.
I am unstoppable and fierce,

I am crystal and stone.

I speak my truth no matter what,
I don't care who disagrees.
I stand tall, even when alone,
I am crystal and stone.

I am a rare specimen of the earth,
I am not so easy to find.
My uniqueness costs the world,
I am crystal and stone.

People try to break me down,
But I will always stand back up.
It is futile to try to destroy me,
I am crystal and stone.

Sleep

As her eyes grow heavy,
They gently
flutter shut.
She morphs into
the unmoving body,
That she was scared
to become.

As her eyes grow heavy,
They see her life
and lies.
All the hidden

parts of her,
Of which she was
terrified.

As her eyes grow heavy,
They see
complete truth.
Nothing more to
numb the pain,
She is no longer blunt
and unmoved.

As her eyes grow heavy,
She's reminded of
her beliefs.
The overarching
pointlessness,
The reason for
Her grief.

As her eyes grow heavy,
Images flash
across her mind.
People who
make her tremble,
That she's long tried to
leave behind.

As her eyes grow heavy,

She thinks of all
she's lost.
The peace of
falling into slumber,
With no worries
and just calm.

Kindred Spirit

"We don't find your breed so often,"
The old man said with a smile,
"But it's always a treat when we do.
Why don't you stay a while?"

I had nowhere else to settle or live,
So, my answer was a resounding yes.
Worst comes to worst, maybe I'll die,
Or disappear out here, I guess.

I clearly wasn't in the best state of mind,
Or the best state of anything, to be candid.
However, these people did seem quite nice,
And I did happen to be stranded.

"What kind of breed is that?" I asked,

As I followed them to their campsite.
The old man turned back and smiled at me,
Eerily comforting in the lamplight.

"That, my dear, is an excellent query,
And there is an answer that is quite plain.
We are the people of kindred spirits,
The ones with depth beyond the mundane."

I felt comforted by the explanation,
Although it was strange and unnerving.
He was correct in his assessment,
Despite his lack of time spent observing.

I realized I wasn't alone out there,
If I felt a feeling, someone else must, too.
Even in the deepest of tribulations,
Others understand what I'm going through.

They situated me in a corner,
It wasn't much, but it was my own.
I had a sense of actual belonging,
I'm home, who would've known?

Later we all sat around the fire,
And spoke endlessly of earth and the sea.
We told happy stories of life and death,
And sang and danced, finally carefree.

I decided then to give in to my essence,
To embody my kindred soul.
It was time to express my genuine self,
And at last, once again become whole.

Nothing

I hear nothing
but
the roar of the wind
and the whisper of the trees
and the breeze in my hair
as the faraway birds
sing to me.

I hear nothing
but
the leaves between my fingers
and the grass under my feet
as the sun calls to me
in the distant
blue sky.

I hear nothing

but
the tall sharp pine trees
and the twigs scratching against me
as the forest shouts
for peace
like me.

I hear nothing
but
the softness of the earth
with the promise of hope
as the seeds beneath
beg for care
and life.

I hear nothing
but
the endless flowing stream
and the coolness on my body
as the strength of nature
covers all of me
head to toe.

I hear nothing
but
someone coming to get me
to bring me back to The Real World
as the leaves gently blow
and the grass rustles

with life.

Wildflower

Be a wildflower
when everyone tells you,
it isn't polite to dress like that,
or stand that proudly,
or speak with so much poise.

Be a wildflower
even if no one else is,

because it's better to stand tall,
and stand uniquely alone,
than to remain a fake sheep.

Be a wildflower
in a world of perfect tulips,
that never have the chance,
to use their voice,
or express their truths.

Be a wildflower
even if you're scared that,
they might cut you down,
for being true to yourself,
and altruistically you.

Be a wildflower
when you feel the weight,
of all the words left unsaid,
on your delicate shoulders,
begging you to be spoken.

Be a wildflower
even when roses are red,
and violets are blue,
because you are so much more,
than the entire rainbow.

Be a wildflower

no matter how many times,
they laugh or tease,
because good things come,
when you don't look back.

Be a wildflower
in your most authentic form,
for when the sun comes down,
and the day is done,
it is just you.

Little Girl

Listen closely, little girl,
To what I'm about to say:
Since you have a tough life,
You'll need to remember this one day.
You're going to grow up,
And it'll be really hard
When all you want to do,
Is let down your guard.
You'll realize you grew up young,
And it really wasn't fair.
Because you don't get to go back,
And relive your share.
What's done was done,
And your childhood occurred.
So don't try to do it later,

Because you won't get un-matured.
But what you need to remember,
Is you have the advantage here.
Because while they're all confused,
Your purpose is crystal clear.
Even though you're filled with pain,
They'll all get there one day.
When they just want to go back,
And know what you know today.
You see that rainbows come from rain,
And sunny days always end,
And no matter how many trees there are,
There still is no way to mend.
You see the truth in the confusion,
Which is no simple feat.
But even if I could close your eyes,
I think I'd rather wait.
For the gift that is within you,
Every time you cry in fear,
Is a blessing that is unique to you,
Every time you wipe that tear.
An authentic existence,
Is not one to be taken lightly.
So when you want to get up and run,
Please sit and hold on tightly.
This won't be your last hard day,
Just like it wasn't the first.
But when I say it will be worth it,
Little girl, trust me, dive in headfirst.

Trust

I don't think you've ever had someone,
Who has stuck by your side.
No matter what happens to you,
I will never leave you.

I love you like family,
I don't care where you go.
Or what you choose to do,
I will never leave you.

You're like a daughter to me,

I will care about you until the end.
More than you can ever understand,
I will never leave you.

I don't care where you sleep,
Or who you sleep with.
I will stay by your side no matter what,
I will never leave you.

I will never stop talking to you,
No matter what happens.
You can trust me,
I will never leave you…

You need to speak to other people,
I can't be there for you anymore.
I love and care about you, but,
I am leaving you.

Old Soul

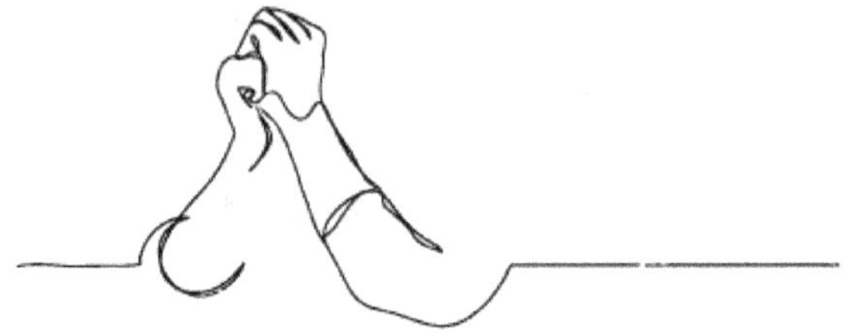

She is an old soul,
With a young heart.
She holds what was,
With what can be.

She is an old soul,
With a lost mind.
She grabs the past,
And lets go of reality.

She is an old soul,
With a skip in her step.
She allows her desires,
To overtake her needs.

She is an old soul,
With a firm grip.
She holds onto her loves,
And releases the rest.

She is an old soul,
With a soft gaze.
She values meaning,
And gives meaning value.

She is an old soul,
With shoulders of steel.
She can carry any weight,
Except for hers alone.

She is an old soul,
With a few sparks inside.
She can explode in a snap,
And fold back up at once.

She is an old soul,
With a twist in her tongue.
She uses it to build,
And to destroy, too.

She is an old soul,
With a desire for truth.
She believes in it all,
Until the very end.

Light

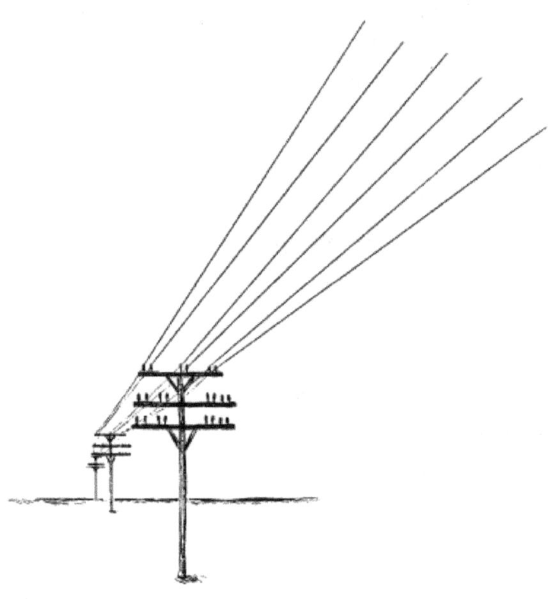

I see a bright light coming at me,
As I stand fixed on the spot.
I came out here to get some air,
But now I seem to be caught.

The inside got overwhelming,
So I walked straight into the street.
I could have gotten hit by a car,
But I just followed the black concrete.

And now this light is before me,

Staring me straight in the eye.
It seems to have frozen me here,
So I thought I should comply.

I'm not sure from where it's coming,
Whether car, bike, or streetlight.
But I know it's quite unyielding,
No matter how long I stare into the night.

It gets pretty underwhelming,
To just stand here and stare.
But I have no other choice at hand,
Since I seem to overtly care.

The light draws me forward,
Just as if I were a moth or a fly.
My eyes tear up as I remember,
There is no single reason to cry.

My life is just a large jumble,
Of "what if?"s and "could it have been?"
When the fact of the matter is,
Nothing happens in pure chagrin.

I finally pull my gaze away,
From the bright, comforting light.
And I walk back to the darkness,
Into the discouraging, dark night.

Royalty

She lifts her head,
and straightens her crown.
Her royalty is breathtaking,
and everyone can see.
She is a vision of fearless poise,
with eternal grace.
Her courage comes
through every strand of her hair.

She lifts her head,
and straightens her crown.

Her spark shines,
with no need for fire to be lit.
She emanates smoke,
and fumes of powerful beauty.
Her mystery sparkles
through her eyes with dignity.

She lifts her head,
and straightens her crown.
Her life is a puzzle,
and she's slowly putting it together.
She is an enigma,
that cannot be understood.
Her problems are like poetry,
and must be tread on lightly.

She lifts her head,
and straightens her crown.
Her head falls each time,
she recognizes her loneliness.
She feels the weight,
of exceptionality on her back.
Her head lifts back up,
as she realizes her uniqueness.

She lifts her head,
and straightens her crown.

Broken

Everyone reaches
their breaking point,
And on that day
she reached hers.
After all the words
and questions,
She snapped
and finally broke.
Everyone reaches
their breaking point,
Is it really a wonder
that she did?
When you really stop
and think about it,
It's a marvel
it took so long.
Everyone reaches

their breaking point,
But she's stronger
than most.
So when she finally
folded and broke,
It contained
a heap of hurt.
Everyone reaches
their breaking point,
And is she
no different than them?
She had enough
of the yelling inside,
As she exploded
and let it all out.
Everyone reaches
their breaking point,
She thought
as she let herself drift.
As all of her pieces
splintered and broke,
She allowed them to
get lost in the abyss.

Believe

He said,
I believe in more
than this world
can comprehend.
He said,
I believe in something
that will make sense
when I see it.
He said,
I believe in a reality
that will cause
the moon to turn faster
and planets to spin quicker.
He said,

I believe in God
even when he can't be seen
because he's shown me
that sometimes he can.
He said,
I believe in a truth
that can be believed
no matter how many lies
make it seem untrue.
He said,
I believe in you
even if you don't
for your eyes are clouded
by yourself.
He said,
I believe in the solution
even when there are none
for there is always an answer
to every single question.

Fly

As I sit looking out before me,
I think, it's worth a shot.
I don't have wings or anything,
But I'll give it what I've got.

I stand and point skyward,
Giving my posture poise and grace.
Knowing full well this could be the end,
Or the beginning, so I brace.

My shoulders contain no wings,
And my back, no magic of flight.
But I feel like flying is within me,
Hidden deep down there, shining bright.

So I take one last look around me,

At the well-grounded rocks, etcetera.
And allow myself the infinite freedom,
Of diving into the abundant plethora.

Something curious happens,
As I shoot down, down, down.
I lose all notions of fear,
As if my courage is renowned.

Then all of a sudden I get lighter,
And my heart begins to fly.
Giving reason to my perception,
When I decided to just try.

Because it doesn't really matter,
What happens in the end.
As long as every single second,
Was spent trying to ascend.